JUNIOR VOCABULARY EXERCISES

C. C. CREW

Revised Edition

Nelson

PREFACE

These exercises are designed to enable brighter children aged nine to eleven to help themselves, and to give encouragement to slower pupils.

The words needed to answer the questions are all given in brackets. The children, by selecting the easier ones first, help themselves to answer the more difficult ones by reducing the chance of error.

Half of the book (the right-hand pages) covers word usage. This embraces about 1000 words. The exercises give a gentle and unobtrusive introduction to the use of words. They should be worked in an ordinary exercise book, and should be supplemented with additional exercises set by the teacher to encourage the assimilation of the new words into the children's working vocabulary.

The remainder of the book (the left-hand pages) introduces a reading vocabulary, which consists of about 400 words chosen from the reading material normally offered to children aged nine to eleven. Words have also been selected from readers issued to seven-year-olds and eight-year-olds. This section is mainly designed to increase the children's ability to comprehend what they read, and to widen their power of interpretation. Some of the more able children will, no doubt, incorporate some of these words in their own working vocabulary. The number of words from this section that may be assimilated into the working vocabulary depends upon the teacher, and on the fastidiousness with which the teacher uses and encourages the use of words at all times.

The words introduced consist approximately of the following: 500 nouns, 300 adjectives, 400 verbs, 100 adverbs, 80 similars and opposites, 35 similes and 20 group nouns.

Taken in conjunction with the vernacular of the average child, these exercises give a well-balanced vocabulary, forming a sound basis upon which to build.

EXERCISE 1

A. Names of things *(male, mail, daughter, female, bundle)*
1. A girl is her mother's ....
2. Letters and parcels carried by the Post Office are called ....
3. A boy is a ....
4. A girl is a ....
5. Things tied loosely together make a ....

B. What kind? *(dark, steep, skilful, nasty)*
1. a .... hill
2. a .... taste
3. .... clouds
4. a .... surgeon

C. What do they do? *(dissolves, cut, wriggles, aches, gallop)*
1. A worm ....
2. Sugar .... in a cup of tea.
3. A bad tooth ....
4. Scissors ....
5. A horse can ....

D. Similars *(girl, shout, try, robber, fast)*
1. *attempt* is similar to ....
2. *yell* is similar to ....
3. *maiden* is similar to ....
4. *bandit* is similar to ....
5. *rapid* is similar to ....

E. Opposites *(stiff, shout, departure, often, disapprove)*
1. *whisper* is opposite to ....
2. *arrival* is opposite to ....
3. *seldom* is opposite to ....
4. *approve* is opposite to ....
5. *limp* is opposite to ....

EXERCISE 2(a)

Find the word   *(wail, claw, wily, precious, caper, bruise, cheap, waist, stumble, disturb)*

1.   The sharp nail on a bird's foot is its c☐☐☐.
2.   If you scratch someone badly, you c☐☐☐ them.
3.   A person who is tricky and crafty is w☐☐☐.
4.   To cry in a moaning way is to w☐☐☐.
5.   Anything of great value is pr☐☐☐☐☐☐.
6.   To jump and skip about in a playful way is to c☐☐☐☐.
7.   If a thing is worth more than you pay for it, it is c☐☐☐☐.
8.   BUT something that is of poor quality is a c☐☐☐☐ thing.
9.   Your belt goes round your w☐☐☐☐.
10. If you nearly fall by catching your foot in something, you s☐☐☐☐☐☐.
11. Dust settles on furniture. When you flick it with a duster you d☐☐☐☐☐b it.
12. When you knock yourself, the swelling that turns black and blue is a b☐☐☐☐☐.

EXERCISE 2(b)

Find the word   *(dismays, nudge, mend, wares, prime, silent, recline, snout, cheat, steal, allow)*

1.   To deceive at work or play is to c☐☐☐☐.
2.   The nose of an animal is its s☐☐☐☐.
3.   To take something that does not belong to you is to s☐☐☐☐ it.
4.   If you let a person do something, you a☐l☐☐ them to do it.
5.   If you poke someone with your elbow, you n☐☐☐☐ them.
6.   Anything that makes no noise is s☐l☐☐☐.
7.   Goods of various kinds are called w☐☐☐☐.
8.   Anything that makes you frightened or upset d☐s☐☐☐s you.
9.   Anything that is first, or top of its class, is p☐☐☐☐.
10. The best meat is p☐☐☐☐ meat.
11. If a thing is broken and you put it right again, you m☐☐☐ it.
12. To lie lazily back at your ease in a chair is to r☐cl☐☐☐.

EXERCISE 3

A. Names of things *(machine, curtain, buttons, cushion, signal)*
1. A .... hangs in front of the window.
2. I rest my head on a ....
3. Mother uses a sewing-..............................
4. A .... tells us when a train is coming.
5. We fasten our coats with ....

B. Where is it kept? *(hangar, garage, kennel, boat-house, stable)*
1. An aeroplane is kept in a ....
2. A dog is kept in a ....
3. A boat is kept in a ....
4. A motor car is kept in a ....
5. A horse is kept in a ....

C. Similars *(thrust, come, lucky, worried, strong)*
1. *uneasy* is similar to ....
2. *push* is similar to ....
3. *powerful* is similar to ....
4. *arrive* is similar to ....
5. *fortunate* is similar to ....

D. Opposites *(pull, freedom, timid, true, constructive)*
1. *slavery* is opposite to ....
2. *bold* is opposite to ....
3. *false* is opposite to ....
4. *push* is opposite to ....
5. *destructive* is opposite to ....

E. What kind? *(shady, shaggy, spacious, lofty)*
1. a .... tower   3. a .... garden
2. a .... room   4. a .... dog

F. What do we do with it? *(mattress, tumbler, paraffin, poker, margarine)*
1. We stir the fire with a ....
2. We sleep on a ....
3. We drink out of a ....
4. We spread .... on bread.
5. We burn .... in lamps and heaters.

EXERCISE 4(a)

Find the word *(stir, muddle, mane, pecks, snare, peg, midget, replace, weapons, shallow, bend, jerk)*

1. Swords, guns and pistols are all w☐☐p☐☐s.
2. When a bird picks up corn it p☐☐☐☐ it.
3. A very tiny person is called a m☐☐☐☐t.
4. Another name for a trap is a s☐☐☐☐.
5. When water is not deep it is s☐☐☐☐l☐☐.
6. The long hair on an animal's neck is its m☐☐☐.
7. When you move the tea in your cup round and round with a spoon, you s☐☐☐ it.
8. When things are mixed up and untidy they are in a m☐☐☐☐☐.
9. Another name for a curve is a b☐☐☐.
10. At school you hang your coat on a p☐☐ in the cloakroom.
11. When you put something back where you found it, you r☐p☐☐☐☐ it.
12. A sharp, sudden pull is a j☐☐☐.

EXERCISE 4(b)

Find the word *(roost, thrive, empty, crunch, harsh, motion, torment, strive, supplies, flounder, amazed, serious)*

1. When fowls go to bed, they r☐☐☐t on a perch.
2. When a thing is moving it is in m☐t☐☐☐.
3. To chew dry things (e.g. biscuits) noisily is to c☐☐☐☐☐ them.
4. To flop about is to fl☐☐☐☐☐☐☐.
5. Anything with nothing in it is e☐☐☐☐.
6. If you worry and annoy someone, you t☐r☐☐☐☐ them.
7. When you are very, very surprised you are a☐☐☐☐☐.
8. To grow strong and healthy is to th☐☐☐☐.
9. When you go shopping for the week's groceries, you get in s☐p☐☐☐☐☐.
10. If you struggle very hard to do a thing, you s☐☐☐☐☐ to do it.
11. Anyone who is rough and unkind is h☐☐s☐.
12. When you are in earnest you are s☐r☐☐☐☐.

EXERCISE 5

A. What do they do? *(alight, squabble, dwell, catch)*
1. Children sometimes ....
2. Passengers .... from the bus.
3. People .... in houses.
4. Fishermen .... fish.

B. How, when and where *(loudly, happily, across, seldom, last)*
1. The children played .... in the garden. *(how)*
2. We could see the smoke rising .... the park. *(where)*
3. My aunt comes to see us very .... *(when)*
4. Tom arrived home .... *(when)*
5. The boy shouted .... to his brother. *(how)*

C. Names of things *(wheels, dandelion, pigeon, meadow, hedgehog)*
1. A .... is a flower.
2. A .... is an animal.
3. A .... is a bird.
4. A motor car has four .... (and a spare one).
5. A .... is another name for a field.

D. What do they do? *(hibernates, sting, spins, traps)*
1. Bees ....
2. A spider .... its web.
3. The dormouse .... during the winter.
4. A spider .... flies in its web.

E. Similars *(cavern, ancient, fall, lean, protect)*
1. *old* is similar to ....
2. *cave* is similar to ....
3. *drop* is similar to ....
4. *thin* is similar to ....
5. *guard* is similar to ....

F. Opposites *(late, backward, fair, answer, spendthrift)*
1. *miser* is opposite to ....
2. *early* is opposite to ....
3. *unfair* is opposite to ....
4. *question* is opposite to ....
5. *forward* is opposite to ....

EXERCISE 6(a)

Find the word *(wicked, prances, pirates, upset, wipe, mock, stray, cruel, gruff, copse, whisk, decorate)*

1. When an animal jumps about on its hind legs it p☐☐☐c☐☐.
2. A person who is always doing bad things is w☐☐k☐☐.
3. A little wood is a c☐☐☐e.
4. To take something away very suddenly is to w☐☐☐☐ it away.
5. If you rub your desk over with a cloth, you ☐☐☐☐ it.
6. To tip something over, or to make someone angry is to ☐☐☐☐☐ them.
7. Men who sail in ships to rob other ships at sea are p☐☐☐☐☐s.
8. You make a thing look beautiful when you d☐c☐☐☐☐☐ it.
9. To copy what someone else does in order to annoy them is to m☐☐☐ them.
10. Anyone who is surly and speaks with a rough voice is g☐☐☐☐.
11. To wander away and get lost is to s☐r☐☐.
12. Anyone who is very unkind and hard-hearted is c☐☐☐l.

EXERCISE 6(b)

Find the word *(hermit, trough, shiver, squeeze, rubbish, neighbours, ancient, tangle, roast, drenched, solemn, inhabitants)*

1. Anything that is very old indeed is a☐☐☐☐nt.
2. Playful kittens often get a ball of wool into a t☐☐☐l☐.
3. If you put a joint of meat into a hot oven, you r☐☐s☐ it.
4. If you get wet through to the skin, you are d☐☐☐☐hed.
5. Anything that is trashy and of no use is r☐☐☐☐☐☐.
6. Anybody who is grave and serious is s☐l☐☐☐.
7. When you shake with cold, you ☐☐☐☐☐☐.
8. All the people living in your street are your n☐☐☐h☐☐☐☐☐.
9. A long narrow dish from which animals feed is a t☐☐☐☐☐.
10. A person who shuts himself away and lives by himself is a h☐☐m☐☐.
11. The people who live in a town or country are called its i☐h☐☐☐☐☐☐☐☐.
12. If you close your hand tightly round a thing, you s☐☐☐☐z☐ it.

EXERCISE 7

A. Names of things   *(elm, granite, chalk, pine, deal)*
1.   .... is a hard rock.
2.   An .... is a tree.
3.   .... is a soft rock.
4.   A .... is a tree.
5.   Wood that comes from a pine tree is called ....

B. What kind   *(faithful, gentle, playful, busy, cunning, savage)*

1. a .... fox		4. a .... bee	
2. a .... dog		5. a .... lamb	
3. a .... bull		6. a .... puppy	

C. What do we do with it?   *(wash, sew, row, eat, drive)*
1.   We .... a boat.
2.   We .... a cart.
3.   We .... with soap.
4.   We .... cheese.
5.   We .... with a needle.

D.   Fill in the blanks

Present	Past	Present	Past
1. travel	....	6. bring	....
2. resist	....	7. bend	....
3. struggle	....	8. teach	....
4. touch	....	9. take	....
5. laugh	....	10. hide	....

E.   Similars   *(back, teach, beer, dear, fisherman)*
1.   *rear* is similar to ....
2.   *angler* is similar to ....
3.   *instruct* is similar to ....
4.   *ale* is similar to ....
5.   *expensive* is similar to ....

F.   Opposites   *(stale, dismount, uncomfortable, teach)*
1.   *fresh* is opposite to ....
2.   *learn* is opposite to ....
3.   *mount* is opposite to ....
4.   *comfortable* is opposite to ....

EXERCISE 8(a)

Find the word   *(rumour, fury, angry, quaint, forbid, mar, mingle, pulp, rod, blade)*

1. Rage or great anger is f☐☐☐.
2. To be very annoyed is to be a☐☐☐☐.
3. To spoil or disfigure anything is to m☐☐ it.
4. A straight thin stick of wood (or metal) is a ☐☐☐.
5. Gossip that pretends to be important, but is rarely true is r☐m☐☐r.
6. The soft sticky stuff inside a berry is p☐☐☐.
7. Something that pleases you because it is so odd is qu☐☐☐t.
8. To mix together in a crowd is to m☐☐g☐☐.
9. The cutting part of a knife (or sword) is the ☐☐☐☐☐.
10. If someone tells you not to do something, they f☐☐☐☐d you to do it.

EXERCISE 8(b)

Find the word   *(prison, ban, disbands, tumble, gurgle, resume, gesture, contorted, adjective, distance)*

1. If you fall down suddenly and roll over, you t☐☐☐☐e.
2. A bubbling sound is a ☐☐☐☐☐☐.
3. To forbid anything altogether is to ☐☐☐ it.
4. When all the soldiers of an army are sent home the army d☐☐b☐☐☐s.
5. If a burglar is caught he is sent to p☐☐☐☐☐☐.
6. The space between two places (e.g. Bristol and London) is the ☐☐☐☐☐☐☐☐ between them.
7. To 'say' something with your hands (without speaking) is to make a g☐☐t☐☐☐.
8. When your face is twisted (perhaps with a sudden pain) it is c☐n☐☐☐☐☐☐.
9. To get on with something again after you have left it for a while is to r☐☐☐m☐.
10. A 'describing word' is an a☐☐☐ct☐☐☐.

EXERCISE 9

A. Where does it come from? *(butterfly, wine, steam, plank, clay)*
1. .... comes from grapes.
2. A .... comes from a caterpillar.
3. .... comes from water.
4. A .... comes from a tree.
5. .... comes from a quarry.

B. What kind? *(squat, rocky, reckless, solitary, destructive, slippery, immense, disastrous)*
1. The .... puppy tore everything it could get its paws on.
2. The lighthouse warned ships away from the .... coast.
3. The ship had a .... funnel that looked as though it had been sat on.
4. The beach was empty except for a .... man.
5. We had to walk very carefully over the .... rocks.
6. A .... railway accident killed many people.
7. An .... pile of snow slid down the mountain and buried the village.
8. A person who takes needless risks is a .... person.

C. Names of things *(ballast, matron, serpent, brood, dimple)*
1. Heavy material (e.g. stones) put in the bottom of a ship to keep it steady is ....
2. A lady in charge of a hospital is the ....
3. A little dent on cheeks or chin is called a ....
4. Another name for a snake is a ....
5. A hen's family of chicks is her ....

D. What is the difference? *(stroll, walk; careful, cautious)*
1. To be .... means to be painstaking.
2. To be .... means to be wary.
3. To .... means to move along without running.
4. To .... means to walk without hurrying.

E. Complete these sayings *(lion, ox, gold, bird, brass, charity, fiddle, lead)*
1. as bold as ....
2. as heavy as ....
3. as fit as a ....
4. as brave as a ....
5. as good as ....
6. as cold as ....
7. as strong as an ....
8. as happy as a ....

EXERCISE 10(a)

Find the word   *(flit, vivid, hatch, rescue, hideous, error, marvel, hate, celebrated, relations, threaten)*

1.   Anything that is very bright indeed is v☐☐☐☐.
2.   To pass lightly from place to place is to f☐☐☐.
3.   A very famous person (or place) is a c☐l☐b☐☐☐☐☐ person (or place).
4.   To bring young birds out of eggs is to h☐☐☐☐ them.
5.   To make secret plans is to h☐☐☐☐ a plot.
6.   Another name for a mistake is an e☐☐☐r.
7.   If you save a person from danger, you ☐☐☐☐☐☐ them.
8.   A very wonderful thing is a m☐r☐☐☐.
9.   To promise to hurt someone is to t☐☐☐☐t☐☐ them.
10. Anything very ugly is h☐d☐☐☐s.
11. If you dislike someone very much, you h☐☐☐ them.
12. Your uncle is one of your r☐☐☐☐☐☐☐s.

EXERCISE 10(b)

Find the word   *(slack, travel, observe, energetic, ferocious, quake, event, brisk, example, precede, scoop, exchange)*

1.   A special happening is an e☐☐☐☐. For example, a sports day is an e☐☐☐☐.
2.   A pattern or a sample is an e☐☐☐p☐☐.
3.   When you make a journey, you ☐☐☐☐☐☐.
4.   To be very fierce and cruel is to be f☐r☐☐☐☐u☐.
5.   If you walk along in front of someone, you pr☐☐☐☐☐ them.
6.   A loose rope is a s☐☐☐☐ rope.
7.   If you watch something closely, you ob☐☐☐☐☐ it.
8.   If you give something and receive something else instead, you ex☐☐☐☐☐☐.
9.   A very active and busy person is an en☐☐☐☐t☐☐ person.
10. To shake like a jelly is to q☐☐☐☐.
11. Anyone who is quick and lively is b☐☐☐k.
12. When you scrape out sand with your hands you s☐☐☐p it out.

EXERCISE 11

A. Who does it? *(carter, tinker, barber, cooper, merchant, plumber)*
1. A .... mends pots and pans.
2. A .... mends gas and water pipes.
3. A .... cuts hair.
4. A .... makes wooden barrels.
5. A .... buys and sells goods.
6. A .... drives a cart.

B. Similars *(comrade, clear, hinder, throw, uncertain, wrath)*
1. *friend* is similar to ....   4. *fling* is similar to ....
2. *doubtful* is similar to ....   5. *prevent* is similar to ....
3. *distinct* is similar to ....   6. *anger* is similar to ....

C. Opposites *(work, undress, master, war, private, nonsense)*
1. *peace* is opposite to ....   4. *play* is opposite to ....
2. *sense* is opposite to ....   5. *servant* is opposite to ....
3. *public* is opposite to ....   6. *dress* is opposite to ....

D. How, when and where *(behind, within, rapidly, soon, sleepily)*
1. The bus left the children .... *(where)*
2. Another bus will come .... *(when)*
3. The kitten opened its eyes and looked around .... *(how)*
4. The notice said, 'Cycle for sale. Inquire ....' *(where)*
5. The man walked .... to avoid being late. *(how)*

E. Fill in the blanks

Noun	Describing word (adjective)	How, when and where (adverb)
1. greed	greedy	greedily
2. scorn	....	....
3. horror	....	....
4. marvel	....	....
5. attraction	....	....
6. hope	....	....

Dictionary work Find these words in your dictionary. Write the words and their meanings in your exercise book.

limit, liquid, consider, sulk, idol, wretch, guide, insure, effect, affect

EXERCISE 12(a)

Find the word *(bucket, cabin, garb, temple, appetite, choke, nibble, scholar, church, chapel, natural, prosper)*

1. If your nose and throat are blocked up, you c☐☐☐☐.
2. Another name for 'dress' is g☐☐☐.
3. Children in school are called s☐☐☐l☐☐s.
4. A very clever and learned man is also called a s☐☐☐☐☐☐.
5. A place where people worship gods is called a t☐☐☐l☐.
6. The place where Christians worship God is called a c☐☐☐☐h or c☐☐☐☐l.
7. A wooden hut or a room on a ship are both called a c☐☐☐☐.
8. A thing with a hooped handle on the top in which you carry water is a ☐☐☐☐☐☐.
9. Anything that grows and is not made is n☐t☐☐al.
10. When you take tiny bites at anything, you n☐b☐☐☐ it.
11. To 'get on' and earn a lot of money is to pr☐☐☐☐r.
12. If you are always ready for your food and eat well you have a good a☐☐☐t☐☐☐.

EXERCISE 12(b)

Find the word *(injured, artificial, decide, decision, manor, squire, catapult, labourer, infects, infection, yeoman)*

1. To make up your mind about something is to d☐c☐☐☐.
2. When you have decided, you have made a d☐☐☐s☐☐☐.
3. Anyone hurt in an accident is i☐j☐☐☐☐.
4. A thing used for throwing stones is a c☐☐☐p☐☐☐.
5. Anyone who passes on a disease to someone else i☐f☐☐☐☐ them.
6. The disease passed on is called an i☐☐☐☐☐t☐☐n.
7. An unskilled worker is called a l☐b☐☐☐☐☐☐.
8. The chief landowner in a place is called the s☐☐☐r☐.
9. Sometimes a squire's house and lands are called a m☐☐☐r.
10. A small landowner (e.g. a farmer) is a y☐☐m☐☐.
11. Anything that is made to look like the real thing is a☐t☐f☐☐☐☐☐☐.
12. Flowers made from paper are a☐t☐f☐☐☐☐☐ flowers.

EXERCISE 13

A. Names of things *(stage, camel, library, cinema, acrobat)*
1. An animal often used to carry goods across the desert is a ....
2. A building where films are shown is called a ....
3. The part of a theatre where the actors perform is the ....
4. A person who does climbing and balancing tricks in a circus is an ....
5. A place where a lot of books are kept is called a ....

B. Where are they made? *(rope-walk, steelworks, power-station, brewery, cooperage)*
1. Steel bars are made in a ....
2. Beer is made in a ....
3. String and rope are made in a ....
4. Wooden barrels are made in a ....
5. Electricity is made in a ....

C. Comparison Fill in the missing words

1.	good	....	best
2.	cheap	cheaper	....
3.	rough	....	....
4.	rapid	....	....
5.	eager	....	....

D. One and more than one
1. one tooth, many ....
2. one potato, many ....
3. one foot, many ....
4. one watch, many ....
5. one berry, many ....
6. one mouse, many ....

E. How, when and where *(heartily, broadly, firmly, yesterday, near)*
1. The man laughed .... *(how)*
2. His friend grinned .... *(how)*
3. John held the bat .... *(how)*
4. By the shouts of the children we knew that the park was .... *(where)*
5. We went to the park .... *(when)*

Dictionary work Find these words in your dictionary. Write the words and their meanings in your exercise book.

bait, backbite, barrier, courteous, collide, dabble, dawdle, covetous

EXERCISE 14(a)

Find the word   *(fad, rind, trim, latch, waddle, mumble, bustling, snug, grope, foil)*

1.   To walk like a duck is to w☐☐☐☐☐.
2.   A person who moves about quickly in a fussy way is a b☐☐t☐☐☐g person.
3.   If you speak softly in a way that people cannot easily understand you m☐☐b☐☐.
4.   A passing fancy or a fussy idea is a f☐☐.
5.   The catch that fastens a door is a l☐☐☐☐.
6.   Anything that is neat and tidy is t☐☐☐.
7.   To stop someone doing something is to f☐☐☐ him.
8.   The peel of fruits is their r☐☐☐.
9.   When you are in a place where you are comfortable and warm you are s☐☐☐.
10.   If you feel your way about with your hands because you cannot see, you g☐☐☐☐.

EXERCISE 14(b)

Find the word   *(fume, dainty, jungle, craze, mute, primitive, extract, invisible, incapable, exterior)*

1.   A dense forest and undergrowth in hot countries is called a j☐☐☐☐☐.
2.   Anything that is very old-fashioned and simple is p☐☐☐☐t☐☐.
3.   If you are very interested in anything, you have a c☐☐☐☐ for it.
4.   To draw or pull out something (e.g. a tooth) is to ex☐☐☐☐t it.
5.   To be silent is to be m☐☐☐.
6.   The outside of anything is its e☐t☐☐☐☐r.
7.   A small and neatly dressed girl is d☐☐☐☐☐.
8.   If something is present but cannot be seen, it is in☐☐☐☐☐☐e.
9.   If you are quite unable to do something, you are i☐c☐p☐☐☐☐ of doing it.
10.   To be very angry and to make a noise about it is to f☐☐☐.

EXERCISE 15

A. What kind? *(brawny, gloomy, splendid, vigorous)*
1. The blacksmith had .... arms.
2. He was a strong and .... man.
3. The windows were so small that hardly any light came into the .... room.
4. The knight rode a .... brown horse.

B. Similars *(sweat, close, throw, error, pull, thankful, grab, aid)*
1. *shut* is similar to ....
2. *perspire* is similar to ....
3. *hurl* is similar to ....
4. *help* is similar to ....
5. *grateful* is similar to ....
6. *drag* is similar to ....
7. *seize* is similar to ....
8. *mistake* is similar to ....

C. What does it do? *(falls, jumps, crawls, beats, flows, tolls)*
1. A frog ....
2. A river ....
3. A heart ....
4. A snail ....
5. A bell ....
6. Rain ....

D. Comparison Fill in the missing words
1. poor .... poorest
2. honest ....
3. elegant .... most elegant
4. .... higher ....
5. .... stoutest

E. Fill in the blanks

Verb (doing word)	Noun (naming word)	Adjective (describing word)
1. play	....	playful
2. wonder	....	....
3. admire	....	....
4. attract	attraction	....
5. compare	....	....

Dictionary work Find these words in your dictionary. Write the words and their meanings in your exercise book.

wrench, wrestle, treasure, turbulent, triumph, stingy, stealthy, staunch, sordid, spacious, escape

EXERCISE 16(a)

Find the word   *(fragile, clump, prank, prod, jumble, prowl, forsake, limpet, exercise, precipice, imaginary)*

1. Anything which is easily broken is f☐☐g☐☐☐.
2. A frolic or a practical joke is a ☐☐☐☐☐.
3. Some animals p☐☐☐☐ in search of their prey.
4. To poke with a stick is to ☐☐☐☐.
5. The edge of a steep cliff is a p☐☐☐☐p☐☐☐.
6. A muddle or an untidy heap of things is a j☐☐☐☐☐.
7. A thick cluster of shrubs, trees or flowers is a c☐☐☐p.
8. To cast off someone and have nothing more to do with them is to f☐☐s☐☐☐ them.
9. A shellfish that sticks very tightly to rocks is called a l☐☐p☐☐.
10. A task set for you to do is an e☐☐☐c☐☐☐.
11. Running, jumping and playing games to keep yourself healthy is e☐☐☐c☐☐☐.
12. Anything that is not true, but made up out of your head is i☐☐☐☐n☐☐☐.

EXERCISE 16(b)

Find the word   *(junction, stolid, ransom, boulder, lout, prickly, automatic, freckle, dispense, sensitive, ruffian)*

1. A large rounded rock is a b☐☐☐l☐☐☐.
2. A lawless, bullying fellow is a r☐☐f☐☐☐.
3. A holly leaf is p☐☐☐☐☐☐☐.
4. A place where two or more roads meet is a j☐☐☐t☐☐☐.
5. A person who is dull and never gets excited is s☐☐l☐☐.
6. A rough, awkward young man is a l☐☐☐.
7. To do without something is to d☐s☐☐☐☐☐ with it.
8. To make up and give out medicines is to d☐s☐☐☐☐☐ them.
9. A small brown spot on the skin is a f☐☐☐k☐☐.
10. Money paid to get someone freed from captivity is a r☐☐s☐☐.
11. Anyone who is easily hurt or made shy is s☐☐s☐☐☐☐☐.
12. Anything that works by itself (like a dishwasher) is a☐t☐☐☐t☐☐.

EXERCISE 17

A. What kind? *(bulky, odious, abrupt, sleek, favourite)*
1. A very nasty and unpleasant person is an .... person.
2. A best-loved doll is a .... doll.
3. A big parcel is a .... parcel.
4. A cat with smooth, tidy fur is a .... cat.
5. A person who does not waste words on politeness is an .... person.

B. How, when and where *(slowly, upstairs, sturdily, inside, now)*
1. The old donkey walked along .... *(how)*
2. He carried the boy .... the house. *(where)*
3. The healthy little boy walked along .... *(how)*
4. He carried the big box .... *(where)*
5. He is glad to have a rest .... *(when)*

C. Opposites *(disorder, go, female, praise, unhook, alive, tight, clean)*
1. *blame* is opposite to ....
2. *order* is opposite to ....
3. *stop* is opposite to ....
4. *dead* is opposite to ....
5. *male* is opposite to ....
6. *hook* is opposite to ....
7. *loose* is opposite to ....
8. *dirty* is opposite to ....

D. Say it in one word *(punctual, punctured, audience, miser, decided)*
1. A thorn *made a hole in* John's tyre.   ....
2. The boy was always *ready at the right time.*   ....
3. The *people at the concert* applauded loudly.   ....
4. The girl *made up her mind* to win the prize.   ....
5. Old Silas was a *man who hoarded his money.*   ....

E. Who does it? *(tailor, cobbler, chemist, farrier)*
1. A .... makes suits.
2. A .... mends shoes.
3. A .... sells medicines.
4. A .... shoes horses.

Dictionary work Find these words in your dictionary. Write the words and their meanings in your exercise book.

canine, canny, brazen, facile, craftsman, solid, nervous, bungalow, fatigue, temporary, permanent

EXERCISE 18(a)

Find the word   *(wedge, embrace, wither, parched, mariner, soar, grimace, overcast, remnant, avenge)*

1. People who are very thirsty indeed are p☐r☐☐☐☐.
2. Land which has been burnt up by the sun is p☐r☐☐☐☐ too.
3. To rise easily and quickly into the air like a bird is to ☐☐☐☐.
4. The bit that is left when all the rest has gone is a r☐☐na☐☐.
5. If you make your face ugly by pulling it out of shape, that is a gr☐☐☐☐☐.
6. A piece of wood or metal which is sharp at one end and gets wider towards the other end is a ☐☐☐☐☐.
7. If you keep a door closed by pushing something underneath it, you ☐☐☐☐☐ it.
8. Another name for a sailor is a m☐☐☐n☐☐.
9. To shrivel and dry up is to w☐☐h☐☐.
10. To hold someone lovingly in your arms is to e☐b☐☐☐☐ them.
11. When the sky is full of clouds covering the sun it is o☐☐r☐☐☐t.
12. To repay an injury done to someone else is to ☐☐☐☐☐☐ them.

EXERCISE 18(b)

Find the word   *(brink, hail, crevice, lounges, cataract, tumult, clamour, melancholy, tremor, contract)*

1. The edge of a precipice, a pit or a river is the br☐☐☐.
2. To shout a greeting to someone is to h☐☐☐ him.
3. Frozen rain is called h☐☐☐ too.
4. A sharp shake or quiver is a t☐☐m☐☐.
5. T☐☐☐☐☐s often come before an earthquake.
6. Anyone who is idle and lolls about l☐u☐☐☐s.
7. Noisy shouting that goes on and on is cl☐☐☐☐☐☐.
8. A very loud noise made up of all sorts of wild noises is a t☐m☐☐☐.
9. People who are gloomy and dejected are m☐l☐☐c☐☐☐☐.
10. A deep crack in a rock is a c☐☐v☐☐☐.
11. A large waterfall is a c☐t☐☐☐☐☐.
12. To shrink and get smaller is to c☐nt☐☐☐☐.

A. What kind? *(vicious, quiet, lazy, gorgeous)*
1. A savage ill-tempered dog is a .... dog.
2. A street without noise is a .... street.
3. A person who will not work is a .... person.
4. A very smart and brilliantly coloured uniform is a .... uniform.

B. Names of things *(convent, corridor, glutton, fugitive, diagram)*
1. A very greedy person is a ....
2. Nuns live in a ....
3. A drawing made to help you understand something is a ....
4. A passage with a lot of rooms on each side of it is a ....
5. Anyone who is running away and being chased is a ....

C. Fill in the blanks

Verb	Noun	Adjective
1. enjoy	....	....
2. apply	....	....
3. please	....	....
4. glaze	glass	....
5. describe	....	....

D. Two meanings *(stick, wax, blow, watch, moor)*
1. A candle is made of ....
2. The moon ....es when it gets bigger.
3. A long twig from a tree is a ....
4. You .... things together with gum.
5. We can tell the time from a ....
6. We .... our team play football.
7. If you hit someone, you give them a ....
8. You .... up a balloon.
9. A large piece of open rough land is called a ....
10. Sailors .... a ship when they tie it to the quayside.

E. Complete these sayings *(nails, church mouse, daisy, mule, eel)*
1. as slippery as an ....
2. as fresh as a ....
3. as poor as a ....
4. as stubborn as a ....
5. as hard as ....

EXERCISE 20(a)

Find the word *(decay, alert, system, elevate, elevator, sinews, spiral, resolute, accumulate)*

1. To become rotten is to ☐☐☐☐☐.
2. If you are wide awake and watchful you are a☐☐☐t.
3. Another name for muscles is s☐n☐☐☐.
4. To collect things together until you have a lot of them is to a☐☐u☐☐l☐☐☐ them.
5. To lift up is to el☐☐☐☐☐e.
6. A staircase that goes round like a corkscrew is a s☐☐r☐☐ staircase.
7. A machine that lifts things up is an el☐☐☐☐☐r.
8. To be firm and determined when faced with difficulty is to be re☐☐☐☐☐☐.
9. A careful plan for doing something is a s☐s☐☐☐.
10. The network of railway lines all over the country forms the railway s☐s☐☐.

EXERCISE 20(b)

Find the word *(encounter, terminate, terminus, criticize, suggest, principal, principles, postponed)*

1. One word for 'put an end to' is t☐r☐☐☐☐☐☐.
2. The end of a railway line or a bus route is a t☐☐m☐☐☐s.
3. To meet someone suddenly face to face (especially when you are not friendly) is to en☐☐☐☐☐☐r them.
4. The head teacher of a school is sometimes called the p☐☐n☐☐☐☐l.
5. Hens, who feed chiefly on corn, have it as their p☐☐n☐☐☐☐l food.
6. Rules that people live up to are p☐☐n☐☐☐☐☐☐.
7. Some people do not drink alcohol because it is against their p☐☐n☐☐☐☐☐.
8. If you say whether you think something is good or bad you cr☐☐☐c☐☐☐ it.
9. Anything that is put off until another day is p☐☐t☐☐☐☐☐.
10. To give an idea to someone is to s☐g☐☐☐☐ something.

EXERCISE 21

A. Where is it made? *(mill, distillery, studio, shipyard, tannery)*
1. Films are made in a ....
2. Flour is ground in a ....
3. Ships are built in a ....
4. Whiskey is made in a ....
5. Leather comes from a ....

B. What noises do they make? *(rustles, jingle, sizzles, hisses, creak, pop)*
1. Coins ....   4. Steam ....
2. Silk ....   5. Corks ....
3. Hinges ....   6. Hot fat ....

C. Similars *(agile, scanty, wide, imitate, damp, wriggle)*
1. *copy* is similar to ....   4. *broad* is similar to ....
2. *meagre* is similar to ....   5. *squirm* is similar to ....
3. *nimble* is similar to ....   6. *moist* is similar to ....

D. Opposites *(rude, frown, asleep, shallow, unscrew, silence)*
1. *noise* is opposite to ....   4. *smile* is opposite to ....
2. *polite* is opposite to ....   5. *deep* is opposite to ....
3. *screw* is opposite to ....   6. *awake* is opposite to ....

E. What kind? *(vast, whitewashed, red, uneven, tottery)*
1. The kitchen was a v........................... apartment with w ....
   walls and a r................................... stone floor.
2. The man tripped over the .... stones in the path.
3. The .... old man almost fell as he walked along.

F. How, when and where *(furiously, bravely, attentively, top, tonight)*
1. The children listened .... *(how)*
2. The fire-engine was driven .... to the fire. *(how)*
3. John will go home .... *(when)*
4. The soldiers fought .... *(how)*
5. The hill was steep, but we climbed to the .... *(where)*

G. One and more than one
1. one perch, many ....   4. one knife, many ....
2. one half, many ....   5. one wolf, many ....
3. one cargo, many ....   6. one goose, many ....

EXERCISE 22(a)

Find the word *(lantern, faint, feint, spring, tease, valour, dealer, scold, regal)*

1. Anything that is king-like is r☐☐☐☐.
2. To grumble at someone who has done wrong is to s☐☐☐d them.
3. A person who buys and sells things is a d☐☐l☐☐.
4. Another word for bravery is v☐l☐☐☐.
5. To feel giddy and weak is to feel f☐☐☐t.
6. Anything that has faded so that you can hardly see it is f☐☐☐t.
7. To pretend to attack one place when you really mean to attack another is to make a f☐☐☐t attack.
8. A box with glass sides in which a candle is lighted is a ☐☐☐☐☐☐☐.
9. To amuse yourself by making someone else angry is to t☐a☐☐ them.
10. A coil of wire that jumps back into place when you squeeze it and let it go is a s☐☐☐n☐.

EXERCISE 22(b)

Find the word *(screen, sandwich, slither, canter, swarm, pitcher, seam, hayrick, echo)*

1. A gentle gallop is a c☐☐t☐☐.
2. A crowd that seems to overflow everywhere is a s☐☐r☐.
3. To half walk and half slide is to s☐☐t☐☐☐.
4. When the sound of your voice is thrown back to you that is an e☐☐☐.
5. A very large earthenware jug is a p☐t☐☐☐☐.
6. The join made when two things are sewn together is a s☐☐m.
7. When hay is gathered in it is built into a ☐☐☐☐☐☐☐☐.
8. Two slices of bread and butter with meat (or something else) between them make a ☐☐☐☐☐☐☐☐.
9. A folding cloth 'wall' that can be used to close off part of a room is a s☐r☐☐☐.
10. The white space on which films are shown is also a s☐r☐☐☐.

A. Fill in the blanks

Verb	Noun (naming word)	Adjective (describing word)	Adverb (how, when and where)
1. succeed	....	....	successfully
2. fool	....	....	....
3. prosper	prosperity	....	....
4. grieve	....	....	....

B. What kind? *(capacious, docile, active, corpulent, raw)*
1. A very big pocket is a .... pocket.
2. A very quiet old horse is a .... old horse.
3. A fat man is a .... man.
4. A busy, lively person is an .... person.
5. .... meat is meat that has not been cooked.

C. Similars *(wander, huge, feeble, plentiful, celebrated, edge)*
1. *enormous* is similar to ....
2. *famous* is similar to ....
3. *roam* is similar to ....
4. *abundant* is similar to ....
5. *margin* is similar to ....
6. *weak* is similar to ....

D. Opposites *(occupied, boastful, exit, expand, somewhere, unjust)*
1. *entrance* is opposite to ....
2. *just* is opposite to ....
3. *nowhere* is opposite to ....
4. *vacant* is opposite to ....
5. *contract* is opposite to ....
6. *modest* is opposite to ....

E. Two meanings *(flag, hamper, drain)*
1. His aunt sent Tom a .... filled with food.
2. Do not .... busy people by getting in their way.
3. Water rushed down the ....
4. Mother puts vegetables in a colander to .... the water off.
5. Flowers will .... if it is hot and they have no water.
6. The Union Jack is the .... of Great Britain.

F. Say it in one word *(oasis, edible, bachelor, ford, gambol)*
1. Sweet chestnuts are *fit to eat*, but horse-chestnuts are not. ....
2. The traveller came to the *fertile place in the desert.* ....
3. My uncle was a *man who had never married.* ....
4. The boys came to a *shallow crossing in the river.* ....
5. Young lambs *run and skip about playfully* in the fields. ....

EXERCISE 24(a)

Find the word   *(rascal, lag, canal, kindle, imitate, laggard, lusty, huddle, murmur, lurk, loiter, embedded)*

1. A scamp or a scoundrel is a r☐☐c☐☐.
2. To lie in wait for someone is to l☐☐☐.
3. When you go slowly, or hang about, you l☐i☐☐r.
4. If you drop behind when walking with friends, you l☐☐ behind.
5. If you are idle and lag behind with your work you are a l☐☐g☐☐☐.
6. A river made by man is a c☐☐☐☐.
7. To be strong and full of life is to be l☐☐☐y.
8. To crowd close together is to h☐☐d☐☐.
9. To copy something, or to act like someone else is to i☐☐t☐☐☐.
10. When you light a fire, you k☐☐d☐☐ it.
11. When something sinks into something else it is em☐☐d☐☐d in it.
12. Quiet talking (a little louder than a whisper) is a ☐☐☐☐☐☐.

EXERCISE 24(b)

Find the word   *(protest, produce, products, divide, division, ignore, legend, variety, frail, spouse, culprit)*

1. Another name for a husband or a wife is a s☐☐u☐☐.
2. A story that has been handed down for many years is a l☐g☐☐☐.
3. A person who is not strong and gets ill very easily is f☐☐☐l.
4. To say you disagree with a decision is to p☐☐t☐☐☐.
5. To take no notice of someone is to i☐n☐☐☐ him.
6. Crops such as vegetables and fruit are called pr☐☐☐c☐.
7. Things which are made such as jam, toys, carpets, etc., are called pr☐☐☐☐☐☐.
8. To split anything into parts is to d☐☐☐d☐ it.
9. Each of the parts is a d☐☐☐☐☐on.
10. A person who has done something wrong is a c☐l☐☐☐☐.
11. A mixture of things is a v☐☐☐☐t☐ of things.
12. A mixture of different acts on the stage is called v☐☐☐☐t☐.

EXERCISE 25

A. Names of things *(ancestors, orphan, luggage, label, pier)*
1. Your grandfather is one of your ....
2. A child with no father or mother is an ....
3. All the things you pack and take away with you when you go away for a holiday are called your ....
4. A wooden roadway on iron or wooden supports running out into the sea is a ....
5. A sticky piece of paper (with your name and address on it) which you stick on your luggage is a ....

B. Similars *(show, slim, pain, steer, pursue, ban)*
1. *anguish* is similar to ....   4. *chase* is similar to ....
2. *reveal* is similar to ....   5. *prohibit* is similar to ....
3. *slender* is similar to ....   6. *guide* is similar to ....

C. Opposites *(fat, give, superior, sweet, hide, seek)*
1. *inferior* is opposite to ....   4. *take* is opposite to ....
2. *reveal* is opposite to ....   5. *slender* is opposite to ....
3. *shun* is opposite to ....   6. *bitter* is opposite to ....

D. What kind? *(pompous, pugnacious, disconsolate, bushy, rustic)*
1. A person who is always ready for a quarrel is a .... person.
2. Anyone who tries to be very dignified is a .... person.
3. The .... boy refused to be comforted.
4. Some men have .... eyebrows.
5. Anything simple and countrified is ....

E. What do they do? *(walks, operates, loads, writes, scrubs)*
1. A charwoman .... floors.
2. A pedestrian .... along the pavement.
3. A surgeon .... on his patients.
4. A docker .... ships.
5. A journalist .... for the newspapers.

Dictionary work Find these words in your dictionary. Write the words and their meanings in your exercise book.

illustrious, illiterate, hypocrite, gangster, furtive, divert, deride, peasant

EXERCISE 26(a)

Find the word *(habit, magic, antic, fortress, shrewd, sincere, choose, respect, chase, bare)*

1. Anything that is not covered up is b☐☐☐.
2. Anything wonderful and astonishing that ordinary people cannot explain or understand is m☐☐☐c.
3. To run after someone and try to catch them is to ☐☐☐☐☐ them.
4. When you pick out one thing from many others, you c☐☐☐s☐ it.
5. If you think well of someone, and honour them, you r☐☐p☐☐☐ them.
6. People who are honest and mean what they say are s☐☐☐☐☐☐.
7. An odd, amusing trick is an a☐t☐☐.
8. A clever person who knows how to get the best for himself is sh☐☐☐☐.
9. Anything you do time and time again without thinking much about it is a h☐☐☐t.
10. A strongly built place defended by soldiers is a f☐☐t☐☐☐☐.

EXERCISE 26(b)

Find the word *(nails, study, discover, wrestle, current, currant, hesitate, settle, crack)*

1. If you pause, and are not sure whether you should go or stop, you h☐☐☐☐☐☐☐.
2. If you drop a plate and it does not break it may c☐☐☐k.
3. To find out something new is to d☐s☐☐☐☐☐ it.
4. Steel 'pins' that you knock into wood are called n☐i☐☐.
5. To work hard finding out all you can, especially from books, is to s☐☐☐y.
6. To struggle fiercely with someone is to wr☐☐☐l☐.
7. To make your home in another town or country is to s☐t☐☐☐ there.
8. Little fruits that you sometimes find in cakes are c☐r☐☐☐☐s.
9. Fast flowing water is a c☐r☐☐☐☐.
10. The electricity that makes electric bulbs light is an electric c☐r☐☐☐☐.

EXERCISE 27

A. What kind? *(strong, comic, mysterious, hasty, wilful, raging)*
1. a .... accident
2. .... antics
3. a .... temper
4. a .... grip
5. .... toothache
6. a .... boy

B. Comparison Fill in the missing words
1. short .... shortest
2. sorry ....
3. simple ....
4. sad ....
5. tame ....
6. stupid ....

C. Similars *(gain, give, odd, disappear, healthy, outside)*
1. *grant* is similar to ....
2. *robust* is similar to ....
3. *profit* is similar to ....
4. *vanish* is similar to ....
5. *queer* is similar to ....
6. *exterior* is similar to ....

D. Opposites *(distrust, sober, crooked, collect, flow, inside)*
1. *straight* is opposite to ....
2. *trust* is opposite to ....
3. *ebb* is opposite to ....
4. *disperse* is opposite to ....
5. *drunk* is opposite to ....
6. *exterior* is opposite to ....

E. Names of things *(venison, constable, conjuror, gauntlet, incubator)*
1. Another name for a policeman is a ....
2. A man who does puzzling tricks is a ....
3. The flesh of the deer is called ....
4. A glove with a wide cuff which you can tuck your sleeve in is a ....
5. Chicks are hatched from eggs in an ....

F. How, when and where *(indoors, steeply, daily, wildly, heavily)*
1. A cold wind made them go .... *(where)*
2. The road climbed .... as we left the town. *(how)*
3. Mr Winkle fell down .... *(how)*
4. The boxer hit out .... *(how)*
5. The old gentleman walked past my house .... *(when)*

Dictionary work Find these words in your dictionary. Write the words and their meanings in your exercise book.

level, committee, flame, curly, arrogant, sneeze, bristles, twigs, ceiling

EXERCISE 28(a)

Find the word *(brass, jade, warden, warder, strew, anchor, scratch, compare, spiteful, haggle)*

1. To argue about the price of anything is to h☐g☐☐☐.
2. A yellow metal made by mixing copper and zinc is called b☐a☐☐.
3. To spread things untidily around is to s☐☐☐w them about.
4. A green stone made into vases and brooches is called ja☐☐.
5. A man in charge of a youth club, or a church official is a w☐☐d☐☐.
6. A man in charge of prisoners in a prison is a w☐☐d☐☐.
7. If you measure one thing against another, you c☐☐☐☐r☐ them.
8. If you make a tear in your skin with something sharp, you ☐☐☐☐☐☐☐ yourself.
9. A heavy iron hook that is thrown overboard to hold a ship steady when it is not sailing is an a☐c☐☐r.
10. Bad-tempered people who like hurting other people are s☐☐t☐☐☐☐.

EXERCISE 28(b)

Find the word *(resist, soothsayer, sorcerer, comedian, desert, loom, weave, fountain, chime, cruise)*

1. To fight against someone who is trying to make you do what you do not want to do is to r☐s☐☐t.
2. A place where practically nothing will grow is a ☐☐☐☐☐☐.
3. When bells are rung to make a tune they ☐☐☐☐☐.
4. A trip on a ship (similar to a coach tour on land) is a c☐☐☐s☐.
5. A man who foretells the future is a s☐☐t☐☐☐☐☐r.
6. A man who casts magic spells is a s☐r☐☐☐☐r.
7. A jet of water that is continuously thrown up into the air is a f☐☐☐t☐☐☐.
8. A man who sets out to make an audience laugh is called a c☐m☐☐☐☐n.
9. To make cloth by working threads in and out is to w☐a☐☐.
10. The machine on which cloth is woven is a l☐o☐.

EXERCISE 29

A. Fill in the blanks

Present	Past	Present	Past
1. break	....	6. forgive	....
2. dig	....	7. ride	....
3. drive	....	8. grind	....
4. drink	....	9. creep	....
5. hear	....	10. stick	....

B. Complete these sayings *(razor, new pin, cucumber, peacock, honey, mustard)*
1. as clean as a ....
2. as proud as a ....
3. as sharp as a ....
4. as cool as a ....
5. as keen as ....
6. as sweet as ....

C. What kind? *(difficult, selfish, frosty, sullen, jaunty, superstitious)*
1. A .... task is hard to do.
2. A .... person thinks it is unlucky to walk under a ladder.
3. The stars are bright on a .... night.
4. A .... child will not share its toys.
5. A .... man has an airy, cheerful manner.
6. A gloomy, ill-tempered person who does not say much is a .... person.

D. Names of things *(calendar, catalogue, waitress, vixen, gasometer, camera, cable)*
1. A table of dates that shows the days of the week is a ....
2. A girl who brings you food in a café is a ....
3. A huge round tank in which gas is stored is a ....
4. Photographs are taken with a ....
5. A list of things for sale is a ....
6. A thick strong rope is a ....
7. A lot of wires bound together into a 'rope' which carry telephone messages under the sea are called a ....
8. A she-fox is called a ....

E. Comparison Fill in the missing words

1. great	....	greatest	4. gay	....	....	
2. thin	....	....	5. much	....	most	
3. many	....	....	6. little	....	....	

EXERCISE 30(a)

Find the word *(worthy, contest, imprint, relic, lever, steadfast, range, subterfuge)*

1. A friendly struggle between people (or teams of people) is a c☐☐t☐☐☐.
2. Something left behind from days gone past is a r☐☐☐c.
3. A person who deserves much respect is a w☐☐t☐☐ person.
4. A long bar that rests on something so that when you press one end DOWN the other end comes UP is a l☐☐☐r.
5. To make the shape of something appear on something else is to make an i☐p☐☐☐☐.
6. Your muddy shoe makes an i☐p☐☐☐☐ of the shape of the sole on the floor.
7. An underhand trick is a s☐☐t☐☐f☐☐☐.
8. A person who is firm, resolute and reliable is s☐☐☐d☐☐☐☐.
9. The distance a gun will shoot is its r☐☐g☐.
10. A large piece of land over which cattle roam is a r☐☐g☐.

EXERCISE 30(b)

Find the word *(mist, vulgar, urge, vagrant, pantomime, verge, drama, beacon, announces, potent)*

1. A cloud of water vapour lying close to the ground is a m☐☐☐.
2. Another name for a tramp is a v☐g☐☐☐☐.
3. A play acted on the stage is a d☐☐m☐.
4. A play made about a fairy-tale is a p☐☐t☐☐☐m☐.
5. Anything rude or common is v☐☐☐☐r.
6. When a headmaster tells the school the result of a cricket match he a☐☐☐☐☐n☐☐s the result.
7. The edge of a grass border is the v☐☐☐e.
8. If you beg, and even worry someone to do something, you u☐☐☐ them to do it.
9. A signal fire on high ground is a ☐☐☐☐☐☐.
10. Anything that is strong and powerful, especially medicines, drink, and spells, is p☐t☐☐☐.

A. The sound is the same *(piece, peace; board, bored; key, quay)*
1. The children were .... because they had nothing to do.
2. A .... is a plank of wood.
3. We unlocked the door with a ....
4. Ships are tied to the .... while they are loaded.
5. Tom likes a .... of cake with his tea.
6. There was great joy when .... came, and the war was over.

B. What kind? *(lonely, hoarse, boisterous, slovenly, squalid)*
1. A child with no friends is a .... child.
2. A wind that is rough enough to blow tiles off the roof is a .... wind.
3. A dirty, untidy person is a .... person.
4. A house that is dirty and never cleaned is a .... house.
5. A rough, husky voice is a .... voice.

C. Who does it? *(dentist, drover, steeplejack, clown, cabinet-maker)*
1. A .... makes furniture.
2. A .... makes people laugh.
3. A .... takes out (extracts) bad teeth.
4. A .... drives cattle to market.
5. A .... repairs church spires and tall chimneys.

D. Names of things *(catapult, horizon, microphone, telescope, earthenware)*
1. Cups and saucers (not made of china), vases and such things may be
    ....
2. The line where the sky seems to meet the earth is the ....
3. A piece of elastic tied to a forked stick makes a ....
4. A tube with glass (lenses) in it that makes distant things seem near is a
    ....
5. The thing that people speak into so that their voice is carried to your radio
    is a ....

E. Two meanings *(maiden, chest, hide)*
1. The part of your body between your neck and your stomach is your
    ....
2. A big box is sometimes called a ....
3. The skin of an animal is its ....
4. To put something where no one else can find it is to .... it.
5. A girl is sometimes called a ....
6. A new ship's first voyage is its .... voyage.

EXERCISE 32(a)

Find the word *(bronze, treat, furniture, spire, trek, shock, whirlpool, whirlwind, ridiculous, prehistoric)*

1. A mixture of copper and tin is called b☐☐☐☐☐.
2. The chairs, tables and carpets in a house are all f☐☐n☐☐☐☐☐☐.
3. Something that existed or happened many thousands of years ago is p☐☐h☐☐t☐☐☐☐.
4. To make a journey with a waggon is to t☐☐☐.
5. Anything that is very stupid is r☐d☐☐☐☐☐☐☐☐.
6. A special outing or entertainment is a t☐☐☐t.
7. An unexpected and unpleasant surprise will give you a s☐☐☐k.
8. A tall tower that rises to a point is a s☐☐☐☐☐.
9. A wind that blows round and round like a spiral is a wh☐☐☐☐☐☐☐☐.
10. Water that whirls round and round is a wh☐☐☐☐☐☐☐☐.

EXERCISE 32(b)

Find the word *(shame, opinion, scoundrel, agriculture, ammunition, sedate, industry, wafted, substitute, atomic)*

1. A calm person who likes things to be just right is s☐d☐☐☐.
2. The miserable feeling you have when you know that you have done wrong is s☐☐m☐.
3. Anything to do with very small particles called atoms is a☐☐☐☐c.
4. What you think about anything (e.g. whether a film is good or bad) is your o☐☐n☐☐☐.
5. A rascal and a cheat is a ☐☐☐☐☐☐☐☐☐☐.
6. Bullets and shells to feed rifles and guns are called am☐☐☐☐☐t☐☐☐.
7. When something is blown along gently by the wind it is w☐☐☐☐☐☐ along.
8. All the work that goes into growing crops and rearing animals is ag☐☐☐☐☐l☐☐☐☐.
9. Another name for work is in☐☐☐☐☐☐y.
10. Something (or somebody) which takes the place of something (or somebody) else is a s☐b☐☐☐t☐☐☐.

A. The sound is the same   *(ring, wring; stair, stare; pain, pane)*
1.   You .... a bell.
2.   You .... clothes by twisting them tightly.
3.   It is rude to .... at people.
4.   You go up the ....s to bed.
5.   Toothache is a ....
6.   The glass in a window is a ....

B. Fill in the blanks

Verb	Noun	Adjective
1. satisfy	....	satisfactory
2. hate	....	....
3. freeze	frost	....
4. shake	....	....
5. delight	delight	....
6. describe	....	....

C. Similars   *(surrender, indolent, glum, pain, curtail, sour)*
1.   *yield* is similar to ....   4.   *lazy* is similar to ....
2.   *shorten* is similar to ....   5.   *acid* is similar to ....
3.   *dismal* is similar to ....   6.   *anguish* is similar to ....

D. Opposites   *(transparent, ancient, nimble, arrogant, wise, genuine)*
1.   *modern* is opposite to ....   4.   *spurious* is opposite to ....
2.   *opaque* is opposite to ....   5.   *clumsy* is opposite to ....
3.   *humble* is opposite to ....   6.   *stupid* is opposite to ....

E. Names of things   *(restaurant, barbarians, linen, nerves, dynamo)*
1.   A machine that makes electricity is a ....
2.   A place where you can buy and eat food is a ....
3.   People who behave like savages are ....
4.   Fibres in your body that carry 'pain messages' to the brain are called
      ....
5.   Cloth made from flax is called ....

Dictionary work   Find these words in your dictionary. Write the words and
      their meanings in your exercise book.

      alligator, ambush, sponge, fault, amplify, slam, rafter, thong, ambulance

EXERCISE 34(a)

Find the word *(erect, glue, feat, proposal, career, trance, fen, exit, emergency, hypnotize, spoil)*

1. If you suggest doing something you make a p☐☐p☐s☐☐.
2. A person who does things as though he is doing them in his sleep is in a t☐☐☐c☐.
3. Horns and the bones of animals are boiled to make ☐☐☐☐.
4. A notable act, such as climbing Mount Everest, is a f☐☐t.
5. Anything that suddenly threatens grave trouble is an em☐☐g☐☐☐☐.
6. To send a person into a trance is to h☐p☐☐☐i☐☐ him.
7. The work you decide to do (perhaps teaching) is your c☐r☐☐r.
8. To damage a thing and make it useless is to ☐☐☐☐☐ it.
9. To walk upright with a straight back is to be e☐☐c☐.
10. To put up a building (or a statue) is to e☐☐c☐ it.
11. The way out of a place is an e☐☐☐.
12. Low marshy land is a f☐☐.

EXERCISE 34(b)

Find the word *(pledge, breach, exist, existence, invention, ray, tomboy, sultry, forecast, pioneer, reluctant, fickle)*

1. Anyone who is changeable and unreliable is f☐☐k☐☐.
2. Another name for a promise is a ☐☐☐☐☐☐.
3. To live and be on the earth is to e☐☐☐☐.
4. Very hot and close weather is s☐☐t☐☐ weather.
5. The person who is the first to do something is a p☐☐n☐☐☐.
6. Another name for life is e☐☐s☐☐n☐☐.
7. A new thing or a new machine is an i☐v☐☐☐☐☐☐.
8. To say what may happen in the future is to f☐☐e☐☐s☐ it.
9. If you are unwilling to do something you are r☐l☐☐t☐☐☐ to do it.
10. To knock a hole in something is to make a b☐☐☐☐h in it.
11. A strong beam of light is a ☐☐☐.
12. A girl who acts more like a boy is a ☐☐☐☐☐☐.

EXERCISE 35

A. The sound is the same *(not, knot; ball, bawl; sent, scent; route, root; ant, aunt)*
1. Cricket is played with a bat and ....
2. To cry loudly is to ....
3. You must .... run across roads without looking both ways.
4. You tie a .... in the string when you tie up a parcel.
5. An .... is a small insect.
6. Your mother's sister or your father's sister is your ....
7. Tom's mother .... him to town to do some shopping.
8. A .... is a pleasant smell.
9. Plants get their food through their ....s.
10. The way a bus goes is a bus ....

B. Names of things *(canvas, group, gloves, owner, island)*
1. Several things together make a ....
2. We wear .... on our hands.
3. A piece of land surrounded by water is an ....
4. If you have a dog of your own, you are its ....
5. Tents are often made of a cloth called ....

C. How, when and where *(successfully, afternoon, warmly, in winter, busily, underground, fearfully, behind)*
1. Miners work .... *(how)* .... *(where)*
2. The surgeon performed the operation .... *(how)*
3. Tom finished his work this .... *(when)*
4. Children are dressed .... *(how)* .... *(when)*
5. The frightened man looked .... *(how)* .... *(where)*

D. Fill in the blanks

Verb	Noun	Adjective	Adverb
1. defend	....	defensive	....
2. force	....	....	....
3. fear	....	....	....
4. protect	....	....	....
5. warm	....	....	....

E. 'Doing words' from animals *(ape, fox, grouse)*
1. To .... someone is to mislead and puzzle them.
2. You .... someone when you mimic them.
3. A slang word for 'grumble' is ....

EXERCISE 36(a)

Find the word *(tense, timorous, transform, tornado, horns, fortune, treasure, token, tavern, gossip, patter)*

1. To chat idly with someone is to ☐☐☐☐☐☐.
2. Anyone who is shy and nervous is t☐m☐☐☐☐☐.
3. Another name for an inn is a t☐☐☐r☐.
4. A symbol or a keepsake is a ☐☐☐☐☐.
5. A violent storm that whips round and round is a ☐☐☐n☐☐☐.
6. A noise like raindrops tapping on a window pane is a p☐☐☐☐r.
7. Money or jewels hidden away so that they can be used later is tr☐☐☐☐☐☐.
8. Pieces of hollow bone sticking out of a cow's head are ☐☐☐☐☐.
9. To change something into something else is to t☐☐n☐f☐☐☐ it.
10. Anyone who is very anxious and worried is t☐☐s☐.
11. If a person has a very large amount of money he has a f☐☐t☐☐☐.
12. F☐☐t☐☐☐ is also another word for 'luck'.

EXERCISE 36(b)

Find the word *(hoist, stampede, troop, tribute, tributary, turncoat, threadbare, fibre, summon, strain, possess, crumple)*

1. A person who is dressed in clothes that are nearly worn out is th☐☐☐☐b☐☐☐.
2. A very thin thread (especially in plants) is a f☐b☐☐.
3. To own anything is to p☐s☐☐☐☐ it.
4. A sudden runaway rush of animals is a s☐☐☐p☐☐☐.
5. A traitor who changes sides is a t☐☐☐c☐☐☐.
6. To make a gift or give special praise to someone is to pay tr☐☐☐t☐ to them.
7. A little river that flows into a bigger river is a tr☐☐☐t☐☐y.
8. To lift something with a sudden heave upward is to h☐☐☐t it.
9. A party of cavalry or a group of boyscouts is a t☐☐☐p.
10. To order someone to come to you is to s☐☐☐o☐ them.
11. To pull with all your strength at something is to s☐r☐☐☐.
12. If you squeeze up paper in your hand you will c☐☐☐p☐☐ it.

A. What do they do? *(directs, mows, graze, converse, migrate)*
1. When people talk they ....
2. A policeman .... the traffic.
3. A farmer .... his fields.
4. Cattle .... in the fields.
5. Some birds .... in winter.

B. 'Doing words' from animals *(dog, hound, ferret, badger, cow)*
1. To follow someone wherever they go is to .... their footsteps.
2. To run after someone and worry him all the time is to .... him.
3. To bully someone until he has no spirit left is to .... him.
4. To worry and browbeat someone to make them do what you want is to .... them.
5. To rummage about searching for something is to ....

C. Names of things *(glider, barge, monument, ferry, leveret)*
1. An aeroplane that flies without an engine is a ....
2. A baby hare is a ....
3. A flat-bottomed boat used on canals is a ....
4. The place on a river (or a narrow sea) where boats take you back and forth is a ....
5. The boat used is called a .... boat.
6. A statue or stone pillar set up to commemorate or honour a famous person is a ....

D. Groups of things *(flock, herd, shoal, bench, fleet, swarm, team, plague, brood, litter)*

1. a .... of sheep   6. a .... of cows
2. a .... of bees   7. a .... of fish
3. a .... of ships   8. a .... of horses
4. a .... of chicks   9. a .... of insects
5. a .... of pigs   10. a .... of magistrates

E. Fill in the blanks

	Verb	Noun	Adjective
1.	quarrel	....	....
2.	talk	....	....
3.	sorrow	....	....
4.	study	....	....
5.	strengthen	....	....

EXERCISE 38(a)

Find the word *(memory, fasten, profit, profitable, metals, idea, fulfil, measure, request, display)*

1. When you ask for anything, you make a r☐☐☐☐s☐.
2. Tin, iron and lead are three m☐☐☐☐s.
3. If you bought something for 10p and sold it for 15p you would make a p☐☐f☐☐ of 5p.
4. Anything that you gain something from is p☐☐f☐☐☐☐☐e.
5. To fix anything so that it will not fly open is to f☐☐t☐☐ it.
6. To make a show of anything is to d☐s☐☐☐☐ it.
7. To find the size or weight of anything is to m☐☐s☐☐☐ it.
8. To carry anything out as you wish is to f☐☐☐☐l your plans.
9. A thought that may lead you to do something is an i☐☐a.
10. The part of your brain which makes you remember the things you see and learn is your m☐☐☐r☐.

EXERCISE 38(b)

Find the word *(released, prisoner, process, writhe, beware, harbour, organize, organization, purpose)*

1. An aim or object that you have fixed in your mind is a p☐☐p☐☐☐.
2. If you do something after thinking carefully about it you do it p☐☐p☐s☐☐y.
3. A place where ships may shelter is a h☐☐☐☐☐r.
4. The special way in which a thing is made is a p☐☐c☐☐☐.
5. Anyone who has lost his freedom and is locked up is a p☐☐s☐☐☐r.
6. When a prisoner is allowed to go free again he is r☐l☐☐☐☐d.
7. To be on your guard is to b☐w☐☐☐.
8. To manage people or arrange things in order to get the best out of them is to o☐g☐☐☐☐☐ them.
9. A group of people who set out to organize other people is an o☐g☐☐☐☐☐☐on.
10. To twist and roll about is to wr☐☐☐☐.

EXERCISE 39

A. What noises do they make? *(bleat, gobble, trumpet, chatter, caw, bray)*
1. Turkeys ....
2. Elephants ....
3. Rooks ....
4. Sheep ....
5. Monkeys ....
6. Donkeys ....

B. Fill in the blanks

Masculine	Feminine	Masculine	Feminine
1. actor	....	6. god	....
2. conductor	....	7.	witch
3. emperor	....	8. bridegroom	....
4.	lass	9.	abbess
5.	widow	10.	nun

C. Similars *(wander, squander, odd, boast, perplex, peaceful, locomotive, enormous)*
1. *waste* is similar to ....
2. *strange* is similar to ....
3. *brag* is similar to ....
4. *puzzle* is similar to ....
5. *roam* is similar to ....
6. *engine* is similar to ....
7. *tranquil* is similar to ....
8. *gigantic* is similar to ....

D. Complete these proverbs
1. Look before you ....
2. .... goes before a fall.
3. Birds of a feather ....
4. More haste, ...
5. Fools rush in where ....

E. Groups of things *(bale, pack, staff, tribe, choir, library, band, flight, clutch, set)*
1. a .... of musicians
2. a .... of servants
3. a .... of natives
4. a .... of aeroplanes
5. a .... of eggs
6. a .... of cotton
7. a .... of wolves
8. a .... of tools
9. a .... of singers
10. a .... of books

F. Complete these sayings *(straight, deaf, bitter, patient, stiff, black, thick, true, hungry, swift)*
1. as .... as a post
2. as .... as a hare
3. as .... as steel
4. as .... as thieves
5. as .... as gall
6. as .... as a poker
7. as .... as Job
8. as .... as a ramrod
9. as .... as a hunter
10. as .... as pitch

EXERCISE 40

Several meanings   *(post, odd, plant, train, scales, fly, bill, peer, bound)*

1. Wooden ....s hold up the fence.
2. We send letters by ....
3. My brother has a good .... in a shipping-office.
4. You must .... hard if you want to be good at football.
5. A .... took us to the seaside.
6. A bride sometimes has a long .... on her dress.
7. A .... is an unpleasant insect.
8. To .... is to go up in an aeroplane.
9. To .... also means to run away.
10. We .... seeds.
11. A .... grows from the seed.
12. The machinery in a factory is sometimes called a ....
13. A strange thing is an .... thing.
14. If you wore a brown coat and waistcoat with grey trousers the trousers would be .... trousers.
15. When a man climbs anything he .... it.
16. When you practise playing the piano, you play ....
17. .... are used to weigh things.
18. A fish is covered with ....
19. A man who is a lord is a ....
20. When you look very closely at something, you .... at it.
21. A bird's mouth is called its ....
22. When you buy something the shopkeeper makes out a ....
23. A piece of land jutting into the sea is sometimes called a ....
24. A jump is a ....
25. When you must do a thing, you are .... to do it.
26. A book is .... when it has its covers fixed on.
27. Places to which you are not allowed to go are out of ....s.

EXERCISE 41

A. Who does it? *(caretaker, cashier, milliner, navvy, jockey)*
1. A .... digs up roads.
2. A .... pays out money.
3. A .... takes care of buildings.
4. A .... sells women's hats.
5. A .... rides horses in races.

B. What noises do they make? *(chirp, coo, clink, croak, clatter, crackles)*
1. Birds .... 4. Pigeons ....
2. Frogs .... 5. Burning wood ....
3. Glasses .... 6. Plates ....

C. What is the difference? *(dirty, filthy; middle, centre; envelope, envelop)*
1. A .... thing is a soiled thing.
2. A .... thing is a very dirty thing.
3. The .... of anything is the *part* that is the same distance from all sides.
4. The .... is the *point* in the middle of a circle.
5. You put a letter in an .... before you post it.
6. If you wrap something up so that you almost smother it, you .... it.

D. Similars *(fatigue, hearth, severe, abode, raiment, adhere)*
1. *tiredness* is similar to .... 4. *fireside* is similar to ....
2. *clothes* are similar to .... 5. *dwelling* is similar to ....
3. *stick* is similar to .... 6. *stern* is similar to ....

E. Opposites *(absent, adult, barren, junior, mad, difficult)*
1. *child* is opposite to .... 4. *present* is opposite to ....
2. *fruitful* is opposite to .... 5. *sane* is opposite to ....
3. *senior* is opposite to .... 6. *easy* is opposite to ....

F. Find the word *(frump, galleon, friar, fry, gnash)*
1. Very young fish are called f....................................
2. To rub the edges of the teeth together in anger is to g.................................... them.
3. A large ship used long ago (1400 to 1700) was a g....................................
4. A monk belonging to a particular brotherhood was a f....................................
5. Monks belonging to the Dominican Order were f....................................s.
6. An old-fashioned, dowdy woman is a f....................................

EXERCISE 42

Several meanings *(spray, size, double, jar, point, hard, rough, seal, store, comb, passage)*

1. Several flowers on one stalk make a ....
2. We .... plants with water from a hose-pipe.
3. Rock is a .... substance.
4. Digging up roads is .... work.
5. Two times anything gives a .... quantity.
6. To .... means to run up and down.
7. A person who looked exactly like you would be your ....
8. To collect things and put them away until later on is to .... them.
9. A shop is sometimes called a ....
10. To .... anything is to give it a sudden shock or bump.
11. You buy jam in a ....
12. To .... on anyone is to irritate them.
13. A .... is a sea animal.
14. To .... means to fasten down.
15. The sharp end of a pencil is its ....
16. To stretch out your arm and finger towards anything is to .... at it.
17. A piece of land jutting into the sea is sometimes called a ....
18. You cannot see the .... of a story when you cannot see any sense in it.
19. Your measurement is your .... in hats and clothes.
20. Powdered glue for mixing into a liquid and painting on walls before papering is called ....
21. You tidy your hair with a ....
22. The red piece of skin on a fowl's head is its ....
23. To search a district for someone is to .... the district.
24. A narrow part of a house that leads from the front door to the rooms is a ....
25. A journey by sea is a ....
26. A piece taken out of a book for you to study is a ....
27. The passing of time is the .... of time.
28. A piece of wood which is not smooth is ....
29. A measurement which is not exact is a .... measurement.
30. A boy who is violent is ....

EXERCISE 43

The sound is the same *(aisle, isle; bare, bear; blew, blue; cereal, serial; meddle, medal; wait, weight; feat, feet; paws, pause; hail, hale; mare, mayor; read, reed; told, tolled; week, weak; fair, fare)*

1. A .... is a big furry animal.
2. If you are not wearing tights or trousers your legs are ....
3. We sometimes eat a .... for breakfast.
4. A story that is told in separate parts week by week is a ....
5. You learn to .... in the infants' school.
6. Tall grasses that grow by the riverside are ....s.
7. People are sometimes given a .... for bravery.
8. If you disturb things without any reason, you ....
9. You .... for a bus at the bus-stop.
10. Your .... tells you how much you weigh (or how heavy you are).
11. A dog has four ....
12. You .... when you stop what you are doing for a few moments.
13. A strong wind .... the tiles off the roof last night.
14. A .... sky means fine weather.
15. A female horse is called a ....
16. The chief man in a town is the ....
17. A man in good health is .... and hearty.
18. Frozen rain is called ....
19. A very fine piece of work is a ....
20. Human beings walk upright on two ....
21. A church bell is .... when some well-known person dies.
22. If your mother says, 'Clean your boots', you are .... to clean them.
23. An island is sometimes called an ....
24. The passage between the rows of seats in a church is an ....
25. There are seven days in a ....
26. If a person is not strong he is ....
27. You pay your .... to the bus-conductor.
28. Anything which is just is ....

Find the word   *(coral, secretary, outlaw, abnormal, cudgel, symptom, sulk, backbite, bait, stingy, staunch, wrench)*

1. A person who sees to the letters of a club is a s......................................
2. Anything that is not normal is ....
3. Anyone who is strong and loyal is ....
4. The material that is put on fish-hooks to catch fish is called ....
5. To say nasty things about someone behind their back is to ....
6. A thick stick that can be used as a weapon is a ....
7. To twist and pull at the same time is to ....
8. A pretty 'rock' made by millions of tiny sea creatures is ....
9. Robin Hood was an ....
10. If you refuse to talk to someone because you are angry, you ....
11. A person who is mean and miserly is ....
12. A sign that shows what sort of illness you have is a s......................................

EXERCISE 44(b)

Find the word   *(auburn, nape, palisade, attic, gable, magnet, cemetery, tannery, caddy, centenarian, core)*

1. The part of the neck between the back of the head and the shoulders is the .... of the neck.
2. 'Red' hair is called .... hair.
3. The little room at the very top of a house is an ....
4. The middle part of an apple is the ....
5. Anyone who is one hundred years old is a ....
6. The tin tea is kept in is called a ....
7. A man who carries golf-clubs for golfers is a ....
8. The place where the dead are buried is a ....
9. The place where leather is made is called a ....
10. A fence made of pointed sticks (often for defence against attack) is a ....
11. A piece of metal that draws iron to it is a ....
12. The pointed end of a house is a ....

EXERCISE 45

A. How, when and where *(loudly, painfully, across, merrily, below, down, quickly)*
1. The policeman acted .... when the man ran away. *(how)*
2. Tom shouted .... *(how)* to his friend .... *(where)*
3. The baby chuckled .... *(how)* as it lay .... *(where)*
4. The man limped .... *(how)* .... *(where)* the road.

B. Complete these proverbs
1. Every cloud has a ....
2. Fine feathers make ....
3. Hunger is the best ....
4. A bird in the hand is ....
5. Fine words butter ....

C. Names of things *(stethoscope, microscope, barometer, megaphone, thermometer)*
1. A .... helps the doctor to listen to your lungs.
2. A .... tells what the weather may be like.
3. People shout through a .... to make their voices very loud.
4. A .... makes very tiny things look large.
5. A .... tells you how hot or cold the room is.

D. Similars *(commotion, labour, havoc, trick, coax, amusement, grasp, disperse)*
1. *work* is similar to .... 5. *ruin* is similar to ....
2. *bustle* is similar to .... 6. *scatter* is similar to ....
3. *clutch* is similar to .... 7. *pastime* is similar to ....
4. *hoax* is similar to .... 8. *persuade* is similar to ....

E. Opposites *(offend, frivolous, disclose, certain, suck, light, assemble, nourish)*
1. *starve* is opposite to .... 5. *please* is opposite to ....
2. *serious* is opposite to .... 6. *doubtful* is opposite to ....
3. *scatter* is opposite to .... 7. *conceal* is opposite to ....
4. *dark* is opposite to .... 8. *blow* is opposite to ....

F. Complete these sayings *(rat, spanner, diamond, bonnet, poke, snake)*
1. to smell a .... 4. a rough ....
2. a bee in his .... 5. a .... in the grass
3. a pig in a .... 6. a .... in the works

EXERCISE 46

A. Complete these sayings *(humble, white, butterflies, wonder, china-shop, flogging, storm, Newcastle)*

1. a .... elephant
2. to carry coals to ....
3. like a bull in a ....
4. .... a dead horse
5. to eat .... pie
6. a nine days' ....
7. a .... in a teacup
8. .... in the stomach

B. Where do they live? *(drey, burrow, lodge, earth, holt, swannery)*

1. A fox lives in an ....
2. A beaver lives in a ....
3. A swan lives in a ....
4. A squirrel lives in a ....
5. An otter lives in a ....
6. A rabbit lives in a ....

C. The sound is the same *(beech, beach; hare, hair; mantel, mantle; ate, eight; gait, gate; guessed, guest; might, mite; hear, here)*

1. The greedy boy .... all the chocolates.
2. Four and four make ....
3. All the strength of a nation is its ....
4. A very tiny creature is a ....
5. The girl has black ....
6. A .... is an animal that looks like a rabbit.
7. The boy .... the riddle at once.
8. When someone comes to stay with you, that person is your ....
9. Put the box ....
10. A person who is deaf cannot ....
11. The sea-shore is called a ....
12. .... is the name of a tree.
13. The way a person walks is his ....
14. You go through a .... to get into a field.
15. A narrow shelf over the fireplace is called a ....
16. A cloak is sometimes called a ....